COUNTRIES OF THE WORLD

GREAT BRITAIN

Anna Sproule

with photographs by Chris Fairclough

Illustrated by Stefan Chabluk

The Bookwright Press
New York · 1988

Titles in this series

France　　　　　New Zealand

Great Britain　　West Germany

Cover *Lunchtime by the Frome River, which flows through the Dorset town of Wareham. Many British people love anything to do with boats.*

Opposite *Parliament Square in London, dominated by the clock tower of the Houses of Parliament. Big Ben is the name of the clock's bell.*

First published in the
United States in 1988 by
The Bookwright Press
387 Park Avenue South
New York, NY 10016

First published in 1988 by
Wayland (Publishers) Ltd
61 Western Road, Hove
East Sussex BN3 1JD, England

© Copyright 1988 Wayland (Publishers) Ltd

Series design: Malcolm Smythe
Book design: Force 9

ISBN 0-531-18157-X
Library of Congress Catalog Card Number: 87-71996

Typeset by Oliver Dawkins Ltd.,
Burgess Hill, West Sussex
Printed in Italy by G. Canale and C.S.p.A., Turin

Contents

All words that appear in **bold** in the text are explained in the glossary on page 46.

1 Introducing Great Britain

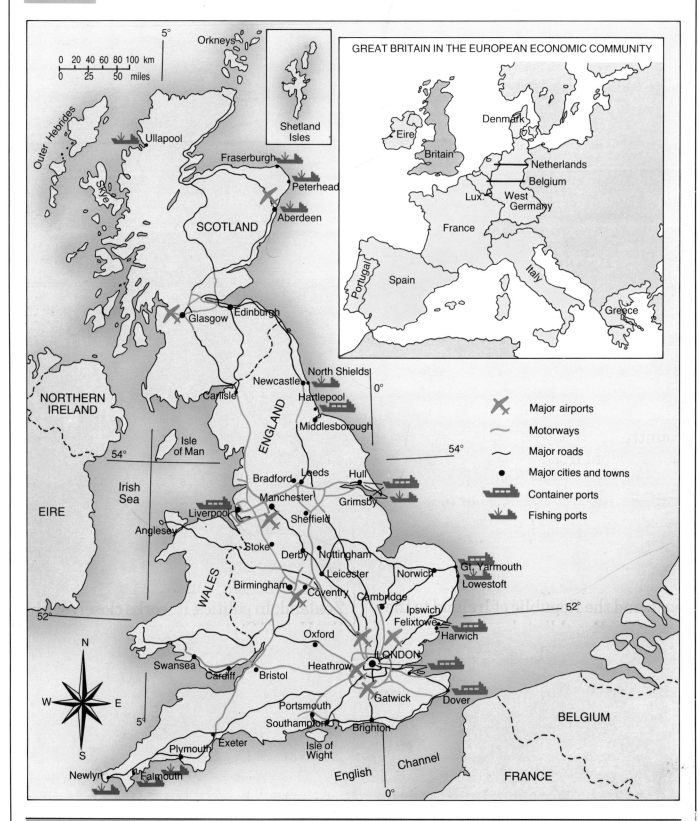

GREAT BRITAIN IN THE EUROPEAN ECONOMIC COMMUNITY

Map legend:
- ✕ Major airports
- ⌇ Motorways
- — Major roads
- ● Major cities and towns
- Container ports
- Fishing ports

Great Britain

Land area: 229,880 sq km
(87,757 sq mi)
England: 130,357 sq km
(50,331 sq mi)
Scotland: 78,762 sq km
(30,410 sq mi)
Wales: 20,761 sq km
(8,016 sq mi)
Population: 54,773,000
England: 46,799,000
Scotland: 5,166,000
Wales: 2,808,000
Capital city: London

Right Gateway to Britain: the port of Dover, seen from the top of its famous white cliffs.

At the westernmost edge of the continent of Europe is a large island with a jagged coastline. It is divided into three different countries that, long ago, used to be independent from each other: England, Scotland and Wales. Today, these countries are joined together to make up a single country, Great Britain.

The sea separates Britain from all its near neighbors. These are the Netherlands, Belgium and France to the east, and the Republic of Ireland to the west. The Republic takes up only part of the island of Ireland and does not include Ireland's northeastern corner. Together with England, Scotland and Wales, this northeastern part of the island makes up the United Kingdom of Great Britain and Northern Ireland.

Although it looks small on a map of the world, Britain is one of the world's fifteen richest countries. Some of Britain's wealth comes from selling goods to other countries, and some from the work it does for them, such as looking after their money (banking). One of the most important goods Britain sells is oil, which was discovered in the bed of the North Sea in 1969.

Britain has strong historical links with many English-speaking countries, such as Canada, Australia and New Zealand. In politics, it works closely with the United States.

In the past, Britain has often disagreed with its European neighbors, and even fought wars against them. But it is now one of the members of the **European Economic Community (EEC)**. This means that Britain now works closely with the countries of continental Europe as well.

2 Land and climate

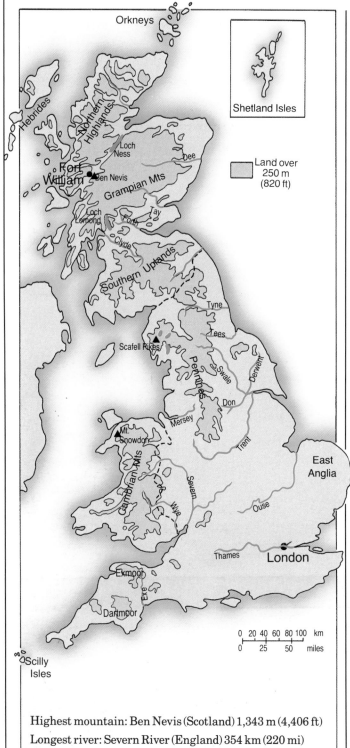

Highest mountain: Ben Nevis (Scotland) 1,343 m (4,406 ft)
Longest river: Severn River (England) 354 km (220 mi)
Largest lake: Loch Lomond (Scotland) 70 sq km (27 sq mi)

Above *Britain's "bread basket": this East Anglian farmer has good weather for his wheat harvest.*

Mainland Britain is divided into two unequal parts by an invisible line that runs at a slant from northeast to southwest. This dividing line starts at the mouth of the Tees River, on Britain's eastern coastline, and ends at the mouth of the Exe River in the southwest.

Most of Britain's hills and mountains are on the northwestern side of this invisible line. The highest one — the mountain called Ben Nevis — is in Scotland, and is 1,343 m (4,400 ft) high. To the south and east, Britain's countryside is generally much flatter.

	London	Fort William
Average annual rainfall	610 mm (24 in)	2,000 mm (79 in)
Average daily temperatures	4°C (39°F) Jan 17°C (57°F) July	4°C (39°F) Jan 14°C (63°F) July

Like most other countries in western Europe, Britain has a "cool **temperate**" climate. Compared to Russia or Brazil, for example, the weather never becomes very cold or very hot. Even in summer, it is rare for the weather to become very dry. Rain is common in Britain all year round.

The shape of the land always has a big effect on a country's weather. In Britain, the wind often blows from the direction of the Atlantic Ocean, bringing damp air with it. When this air reaches hills or mountains, the dampness in it turns into rain. So the northwestern, hilly half of Britain is wetter than the southern, flatter half. (The west also has a milder climate than the east. This is caused by the Gulf Stream, a warm ocean current off Britain's western shores.)

During winter, rain can often fall as snow in Scotland and northern England. The south and east, however, can also become very cold, with winds blowing from Europe bringing snow.

Snow-covered mountains in the Inner Hebrides. Winter comes early to Scotland.

3 Wildlife

The mixture of moderate temperatures and frequent rain has given Britain a rich natural environment. The many different **habitats** include heath and moorland, marshes and woodland.

Hundreds of years ago lowland Britain was covered with woodland. Since then, the British countryside has been changed by generations of farmers. But, if all farming stopped tomorrow, the land would gradually go back to its natural state — woodland. Oak, beech and ash are the most common trees of England's remaining natural forests. In Wales, birch is also common, while the main forest trees of Scotland are birch and pine.

Above The robin, Britain's national bird, is a common garden visitor in winter.

Below Otters like these are getting scarcer and scarcer. They are now being specially bred and returned to the wild.

With his herd behind him, a big fallow deer shows off his magnificent antlers.

Woodlands support a huge number of plant and animal species, especially if plenty of light and air can reach the forest floor. It has been calculated that an oak can offer food to almost 200 different kinds of caterpillars. Many **mammals** live in the woods, too, ranging in size from deer to tiny woodmice.

Although most of Britain's forest has been turned into farmland, narrow strips of woodland survive as hedges. These also support a rich wildlife. But the creatures that live in them are living in danger, because many British farmers dig up hedges to make bigger fields.

New houses and roads are being built all the time, and this destroys the natural habitat as well. Industrial **pollution** is also destructive. Today, some of Britain's animals, birds, insects and plants are becoming so rare that they are in danger of becoming **extinct**.

The barn owl is now very rare in Britain because much of its natural habitat has been destroyed.

4 History

Although Britain is an island, it is close to mainland Europe and easy to reach by sea. In very early times the Romans came to Britain. They were attracted by mineral wealth, especially by lead, copper and gold. Later invaders came in search of new lands to farm and new territories to rule. Many other people came to Britain to be safe from their enemies. Over the years, people have also left Britain for foreign lands. These comings and goings have been important in shaping Britain's history.

People have left Britain for many reasons. British explorers crossed the Atlantic Ocean, sailed around the world, ventured into the Arctic, and explored the coast of Australia. British businessmen took British goods abroad. British soldiers kept control over Britain's huge overseas empire.

But some people left Britain not to make fortunes but to find freedom. Some did not like its religion. In 1620, for instance, a group called the Pilgrims made the very dangerous journey across the Atlantic Ocean to settle in North America. There they could worship as they wanted to.

Below A scene from the Bayeux Tapestry showing King Harold of England and William of Normandy, who defeated him in 1066. This was the last time that a foreign invader set foot on mainland Britain.

In the late seventeenth century, Britain began to change its farming methods. Farmers started to figure out ways of making their land produce more food. This change was called the "Agricultural Revolution."

Heavy industry was also a British invention, and so were factories. It was the British who, in the late 1700s, first figured out how to use steam and water to drive machines. Their discovery started what is called the "**Industrial Revolution**." Until then, most people had worked at home. Now they worked in the factories that housed the new machines. The country became rich on what they made.

Above In 1620 the Pilgrims set sail for North America in their ship the Mayflower.

Right Making steel in Newcastle upon Tyne. The picture includes many of the other products of the Industrial Revolution.

In the nineteenth century Britain became the greatest industrial country in the world. But some people did not share in the wealth the Industrial Revolution brought. Thousands of Scots, for example, were turned off the lands they farmed and had to seek new homes overseas. Many workers in cities were desperately poor. Poor people who broke the law were very harshly treated. Many were sent as a punishment to Australia, which was then a British **colony**.

Right The Last of England: *a nineteenth-century painting by Ford Madox Brown that shows a young couple and their baby emigrating to Australia.*

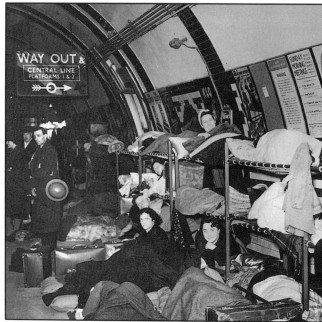

Above During World War II (1939–45), Londoners slept in the subway stations to be safe from bombs.

Left The scene that Londoners woke up to on many mornings of the war: the damage caused by a bombing raid.

In the twentieth century more big changes have taken place. The British Empire no longer exists. This is because most British colonies have become independent. However, they now form part of the **Commonwealth**, of which Queen Elizabeth II is the head, and so strong links with Britain still remain. Since 1945, many British people have chosen to go to Australia, New Zealand and Canada to seek work and a better way of life.

Athletes from all Commonwealth countries may compete in the Commonwealth Games, which are held once every four years. In 1982, the Games were held in Brisbane, Australia. Here, Steve Cram of Britain (left), Mike Boit of Kenya and John Walker of New Zealand compete in the 1,500 m race.

Important dates

55 B.C.	The Romans invade Britain
A.D. 410	The Romans leave; later, parts of Britain occupied by invaders from Northern Europe, such as the Saxons and Vikings.
802	Egbert becomes the first king of all England.
1066	William of Normandy invades and conquers England.
1282	Wales gives in to Norman rule.
1536	Act of Union joins England and Wales.
1558	Queen Elizabeth I of England comes to the throne. During her reign England becomes the most powerful country in Europe.
1642-8	The Civil War.
1649	King Charles I is beheaded. England and Wales become a **republic**.
1660	The monarchy is restored.
1700s	Agricultural Revolution. Great improvements in farming methods.
1707	Act of Union joins Scotland to England and Wales to become Great Britain.
Mid 1700s	Industrial Revolution starts. Over the next century Britain becomes the greatest industrial nation in the world.
1837-1901	Queen Victoria's reign.
1914-18	World War I. Britain, France and Russia join to fight Germany and Austria. Germany is beaten, but over one million British troops are killed.
1928	All women given the vote.
1939-45	World War II. Nazi Germany, Italy and Japan are beaten by the **Allies**.
1944	Education Act provides free secondary education for all.
1969	Discovery of oil in the North Sea.
1973	Britain joins the EEC.

5 The British today

Above *A shopping area in the London suburb of Southall, where many people live whose families originally came from India and Pakistan.*

Great Britain is a densely populated country. Over 54 million people live within its 229,880 sq km (88,757 sq mi) — an average population of about 570 people per square mile.

But some areas of Britain are more crowded than others. The southeastern corner, for instance, is much more densely populated than the southwest. Wales, Scotland and parts of northern England have large areas that are very thinly populated indeed. Here, there are fewer than sixteen people living in each square mile.

The most crowded places in Britain are its big cities, and especially its capital, London. But more and more people are now begining to leave the cities to live in the **suburbs**, in housing developments called "new towns," or in the country. So London's population is falling, and so is that of the other big cities.

Although they all belong to one nation, the people of Great Britain come from many different lands. They may be English, Scottish, Welsh or Irish, or their families may have come to Britain from overseas.

In the 1950s, British people from Commonwealth countries such as India, Pakistan and parts of Africa and the Caribbean, were encouraged to move to Britain. In those days there were plenty of jobs for everyone. Britain has also provided a home for **refugees**.

In Britain nearly everyone speaks English, although the accent may vary in different regions. But other languages are spoken too. In the Scottish Highlands and islands, Gaelic is spoken. In Wales, one in five of the population speaks Welsh. People who have come to Britain from other countries may be **bilingual**, and speak their own language as well as English.

Above A Welsh schoolgirl reads a book in Welsh, which is very different from the English language.

Below A senior citizen tends his garden. The number of elderly people in Britain is growing fast.

6 Cities

For four out of every five people in Britain, home is somewhere in a city or town. There are usually more jobs for people in cities than there are in country areas. There are more stores, and a wider range of goods in them. The schools are bigger, and this means they can teach a lot of different subjects. There is more to do in the evenings and on weekends as well. Most of Britain's cities and towns have grown up near the coast or in lowland areas near the coalfields. They are shown on the map on page 4.

Wales and Scotland have their own capital cities, Cardiff (Wales) and Edinburgh (Scotland), but the capital of Great Britain is London on the Thames River. London has been the most important city in Britain since Roman times. It now covers an area of more than 960 sq km (370 sq mi) and has a population of over 6 million. Central London is full of famous landmarks, both old and new. These sights, together with theaters, concert halls, art galleries and museums, attract thousands of tourists

Edinburgh, capital of Scotland, here seen with Edinburgh Castle in the mid-distance.

Above Homes in inner London. Most Londoners prefer houses to apartment blocks, even if the apartments are newer.

Above St. David's Hall, a new concert hall and arts center in Cardiff, capital city of Wales.

each year. Britain's other cities also have much to offer.

Although most jobs tend to be in the city centers, many people prefer to live in the suburbs. This means that they spend a lot of time traveling to and from work each day. In London, the railroad stations, the tube (underground railroad), buses and sidewalks are crowded with these **commuters** during the daily "rush hours."

Britain's cities have problems as well as attractions. The building of new houses and apartments in the suburbs often means that old housing in the city center falls into decay. Many cities, such as Glasgow, Newcastle upon Tyne and Liverpool, have suffered badly from the decline of heavy industries such as shipbuilding. This has resulted in high unemployment and poverty. However efforts are now being made to improve decaying city centers and docklands. Leith (Edinburgh's ancient port), and Glasgow, for example, are encouraging light industry and small businesses.

7 The family at home

According to a traditional British saying, "An Englishman's home is his castle." The Scots and the Welsh feel much the same way. It means that, whatever may happen to them in the world outside, the British see their homes as their own tiny kingdoms.

Until about 40 years ago, most people in Britain rented their houses. Today, over three-quarters of the population hope to buy homes of their own, and six households out of every ten now do. This makes home ownership much more widespread in Britain than in western Europe.

Left Making a scone — a sort of fruit bread — for the family's tea. Many boys enjoy cooking.

Below A summer weekend at home.

Time for homework, and this schoolgirl spreads her books out on her desk.

Almost half the houses in Britain have been built in the last 40 years. Most British are very proud of their homes. Many spend time and money on do-it-yourself improvements. If possible they like to have a garden as well. People without a garden may rent an allotment — a plot of land on which to grow vegetables.

Families themselves have also changed over the last 40 years. One of the biggest changes has been in the part played in family life by women. In Britain, it is now quite unusual to find a "traditional" family — one in which the husband goes out to work and the wife stays at home, looking after the children. Today, almost two-thirds of married women in Britain have jobs, and high unemployment sometimes means that a father takes over the job of looking after the children while his wife is out working.

8 Growing up in Britain

From Mondays to Fridays, a British child's day usually starts somewhere between half-past six and eight in the morning. Between these times, over half the British population gets up. A few people get up much later — but that is usually because they have no children to get to school!

British children have to be at school around 9:00 a.m. The school day lasts over six hours, but children don't spend the whole time in class. There are breaks for play and a longer break for lunch. If they live nearby, pupils can go home for lunch. Otherwise, they eat at school. Whichever they do, what they eat is sure to include plenty of potato chips called "crisps" in Britain. French fries, too, are among British children's favorite food. Foods like hamburgers and sausages are almost as popular. However, healthier eating habits are now being encouraged. Many parents, and schools, are providing meals that are less sugary and less fatty.

A lollipop man — named after his lollipop-shaped sign — helps children cross the road to school.

Above *After school. Three of these girls are off to enjoy themselves. The fourth is earning money on a paper route.*

Right *Writing a letter is fun if you can do it on your own home computer.*

The clothes British children wear at school are much less formal than they used to be. Often, school uniform is just a shirt and trousers or skirt in the school's special colors. At home, both boys and girls wear casual clothes like jogging suits, jeans, parkas and running shoes.

Older children have homework to do in the evening, but they also watch television or listen to records and tapes. They may enjoy sports or go to a movie or disco on weekends. Most younger children are free to do what they like in the evenings and watch television or a video cassette or play with friends.

9 Education

At the age of five, all British children have to start their education. A few are taught by their parents at home, but most of them go to school. British law says that they must stay in school until they are 16.

Most children go to elementary school until they are 11 (or 12 in Scotland, where the law is slightly different). In elementary school, each class has its own teacher. Usually, that teacher stays with the class for all its lessons. In the morning, for example, the teacher might get the class working on math, with the school computer. After a break for recess around 11 o'clock, the class might be asked to write stories; while this is going on, the teacher will hear different children read. Most schools hold an "assembly" every day, when the children sing hymns and pray.

At 11 or 12, British children change schools and go to secondary school. Most secondary schools are "comprehensives." Each takes children of all abilities from a particular area. Secondary schools have different teachers for each subject. After school, pupils have homework to do. Many of the older ones take national examinations in their last year.

Although pupils can leave school at 16, some stay on for another two years to do more work and study for exams. If they do well, they can go on to colleges or universities. In London and Scotland, almost half the secondary school pupils decide to stay on.

Left Elementary schoolchildren celebrating harvest festival at their school assembly.

British parents do not have to pay for their children's education. The money to pay for it comes from **rates and taxes**. However, some parents choose to send their children to fee-paying private schools. "Prep" (preparatory) schools take children from the ages of 8 to 13. Then they go to a "public" school. Many pupils will be boarders, which means they live at school during the school term.

Below A music lesson in a secondary school: a pupil tries out an electronic keyboard.

10 Shopping

In a village everyone knows everyone else, and enjoys a chat at the village store.

Where do the British like to shop? For ordinary shopping — to buy the family's food, for example — the shopper will head for stores that are nearby, or cheap, or both. In towns and cities, this will be a self-service supermarket. But out of the town center its place is taken by the small neighborhood grocery, or "corner shop." In a country district, this may be a village stores that sells everything from potatoes to bootlaces.

Open-air markets and supermarkets sell things more cheaply than small stores can. Supermarket shopping is also quick, since everything is sold under one roof. Because of this, many British shoppers prefer them to ordinary stores. But even people in a hurry will say that it is more pleasant to shop in a British village store or corner shop because they can chat with the storekeeper and exchange news with other customers.

Department stores (large stores selling all kinds of goods including clothes, furniture and hi-fi equipment) now have some new rivals in "superstores" and "hypermarkets." These are being built at out-of-town shopping centers — there may be huge supermarkets, a do-it-yourself (DIY) center, and furniture and carpet showrooms. One huge new shopping mall, called Metrocentre, has been built on 100 acres of wasteland.

Above *All over Britain, the milkman is part of the early-morning scene as he delivers milk to each doorstep.*

Left *You can always find a bargain at an outdoor sale, where people turn their cars into market "stalls."*

Below *British currency and stamps. One pound (£) is divided into 100 pence (p).*

The British are fond of "window shopping": wandering around the centers of their big cities, admiring the beautiful window displays in the stores. Another sort of shopping they love is hunting for bargains at sales, when stores sell off their goods cheaply. To make sure of getting what they want, some customers will stay up all night, waiting on the sidewalk outside the store for the sale to start.

British food

Bacon and eggs, Christmas pudding, Welsh rarebit, gooseberry fool, steak-and-kidney pie, black bun and Stilton cheese are just a few of the traditional foods of Britain. Their tastes contradict the idea that British food is boring. So do their names! (Welsh rarebit is toasted cheese, "fool" is a cold pudding, and "black bun" is a rich Scottish cake.)

For visitors to Britain, the grand British breakfast — with eggs, bacon, sausages, tomatoes, fried potatoes — is probably the most popular dish. But, like much of Britain's traditional menu, it is complicated to prepare and solid to eat. The British themselves are switching from their fried breakfasts to something lighter and healthier, like cereals.

A typical British breakfast today: cereals and a cup of tea.

Above Originally from the United States, McDonald's "take-aways" can now be found in most British towns.

The same thing is happening with the rest of the day-to-day British menu. On the average, people now eat less of the foods that have fat in them, like butter, and they are drinking less milk. Instead of red meat (which also has fat in it), they are eating more poultry and fish.

They are also eating many more foods and dishes introduced by people who come to Britain from all over the world. There are Italian pizzas, American hamburgers, and even the smallest town now has its Indian, Pakistani and Chinese restaurants that sell "**take-aways**" (take-out food).

In spite of all these changes, there is one thing in the British diet that hasn't changed at all. Although many young people now drink coffee, the traditional drink of Britain is tea — and the British still buy more tea than anyone else in the world.

Below Some of Britain's famous regional cheeses.

12 Sports and leisure

Above *Fishing is a favorite sport with many boys.*

Below *Vacationers on Brighton beach. People flock to Britain's seaside towns on sunny summer days.*

Britain is a nation that enjoys sports. The favorite sport is walking, closely followed by snooker, a variety of pool. Other favorites are fishing, swimming, yoga, darts, soccer (which the British call football) and golf. In the past few years there has been great interest in fitness and outdoor activities.

Many people, especially men, like watching sports on television. But for everyone, watching television beats everything else as the thing they like doing best in their leisure time. Three-quarters of the population watch it once their evening meal is over, and almost half watch it before, as well. Television has also created an interest in "new" sports, such as American football.

Above The end of the day: three of the family watch TV, two play, and one reads.

Left A huge ginger cat purrs under the attentions of two young pet-lovers.

If the British don't watch a television program, they often read, listen to music, or go out to meet their friends at a public house or "pub." Some may go to the movies instead. But, thanks to video cassettes and take-out food, people can now have a "night out at the movies" at home — and many do.

The British are famous for having pets — from sheep to walking-stick insects and from cockatoos to snails. The most popular pet in Britain is the dog. Over a quarter of the British own at least one. This may be the reason why walking is the top British sport! A survey done in 1986 showed that the people who particularly like dogs are often in their teens or early twenties. Cats are also favorites, especially with people who are older or live in smaller homes.

13 GREAT BRITAIN
Religion and festivals

Above It's nearly Christmas and these schoolchildren rehearse for the end-of-term Nativity play.

In Britain, the main religion is Christianity. Today, fewer people go to church than in the past, and only one person out of every seven is a practicing Christian. But the British year is still divided up by ancient Christian festivals, such as Christmas and Easter. Whatever their beliefs, most British enjoy these as holidays.

They also enjoy taking part in all the festival traditions. At Christmas, for instance, people go from house to house singing **carols** and collecting money for

Above A Jewish family celebrating the Sabbath.

charity. Children hang stockings or pillowcases at the foot of their beds, which they find filled with presents on Christmas morning. Easter is the time for decorated eggs or chocolate eggs.

Some British have different

religious beliefs. The people who have come to Britain from other countries may still follow their own religions. They include Jews, Muslims, Sikhs and Hindus. For Jewish people, December is the month for Hanukkah, a festival with origins in ancient Jewish history. For Muslims, a day in December marks the start of the Islamic New Year. Sikhs have an important day in December, too. It marks the death of one of their holiest men, 300 years ago.

Religious beliefs

Christians:	Followers
Roman Catholics	2,000,000
Church of England	2,000,000
Church of Scotland	900,000
Methodists	500,000
Baptists	226,000

Other religions:	
Islam	900,000
Sikhism	175,000
Hinduism	140,000
Judaism	111,000

Below British Hindus celebrate the autumn festival of Diwali in the traditional Hindu way.

14 Customs and traditions

Most areas in Britain have their own special foods, their own special ways of building houses, even their own special songs and dances. These things are regional traditions: customs that people have followed for a long time. In some places, these customs have almost been forgotten but, in others, people take pride in keeping them alive.

Above *This Scots family have cooked haggis to celebrate Burns Night.*

Left *People used to shower a British bride and groom with rice. Now they throw paper confetti.*

Below *One of Britain's newest and most colorful traditions, the Notting Hill Carnival, takes place in London each summer. This girl is wearing a spectacular Caribbean costume.*

On January 25 the Scots celebrate Burns Night. This was the birthday of Robert Burns (1759—96), a famous Scottish poet. On this night it is traditional to eat **haggis**, which is brought to the table to the sound of bagpipes.

Below Bonfire Night, November 5, when many people have fireworks parties.

There are some customs that people follow wherever they live in Britain. If you ask them what they'll be doing on November 5, they'll start talking about bonfires and fireworks. This is Bonfire Night, when people remember the man who tried to blow up the Houses of Parliament in 1605. His name was Guy Fawkes. Today, people burn life-sized dummies called "guys" on their bonfires.

15 Culture and the arts

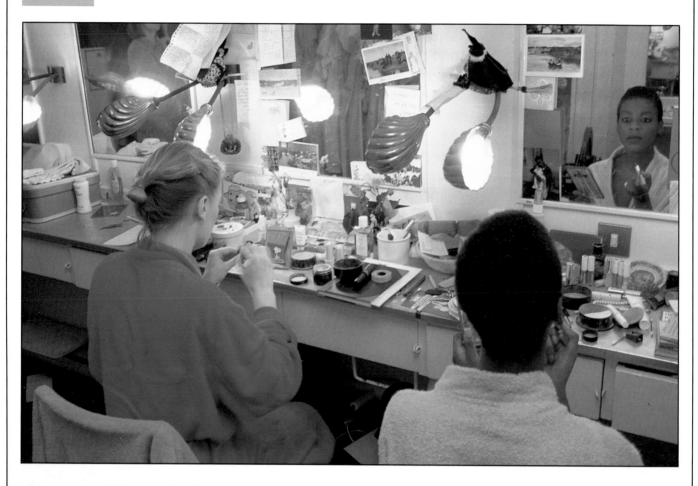

People visit Britain for many reasons. Some come to work and some come to learn the language. Most of the people who come for a holiday want to experience Britain's culture. What does this mean?

For theater-goers, it means seeing the plays of Britain's greatest playwright, William Shakespeare. London alone has more than fifty theaters. But they may go and see musicals like *Cats* or *The Phantom of the Opera* as well. For visitors watching television in their hotel rooms, there are world-famous programs like *Coronation Street* and *EastEnders*.

Above *Actresses of the Royal Shakespeare Company apply makeup before going on stage.*

Music lovers have plenty to please them, too. Britain is full of concert halls, and the British calendar is crowded with music festivals held all over the country. Much of the music audiences hear was composed in Britain, from eighteenth-century composers like Handel to recent composers like Lennon and McCartney. Young Britons enjoy (and produce) some of the best pop music in the world. Older people turn up in thousands to sing in choirs, play in brass bands, or watch the works of Britain's best loved writer-composer team of the nineteenth century, operetta writers Gilbert and Sullivan. Wales is especially famous for its music. Every year there is an international music festival held in North Wales called the Eisteddfod.

For people who like to look rather than listen, there's a lot to look at. There are churches like St. Paul's Cathedral in London, stately homes like Blenheim Palace, and castles such as Edinburgh Castle and Caernarvon Castle. There are great works of art in galleries and museums, and lively paintings by modern artists on the walls of buildings.

Right The Royal National Eisteddfod of Wales, a famous music and poetry festival, is held once a year.

Pipe music and Scottish dancing attract the crowds to the annual Highland Games at Braemar, Scotland.

16 Farming and fishing

Legend

- 🐂 Dairy cattle
- 🐄 Beef cattle
- 🐑 Sheep farming
- 🌾 Cereals
- 🍎 Fruit
- 🥬 Vegetables
- 🐟 Fishing

Surrounded by melting snow, a border collie herds sheep for a Welsh hill farmer.

Although Britain is a crowded country, its farmers still manage to produce over half the food the British need. They do it by using ultra-modern farming methods and equipment. Britain's agricultural industry is one of the most efficient in the European Economic Community.

The kind of food British farmers produce depends on the climate and the type of land they farm. England's biggest croplands are in the flatter, eastern, half of the country. Here, great fields of wheat, barley or sugar beets can stretch almost to the horizon.

Farmers in the east do keep some cattle and sheep for milk and meat, but the big livestock areas of Britain are in the west. The southwest is especially famous for dairy products, such as Devonshire cream, traditional Cheddar cheese from Somerset, and the rich milk produced by Jersey and Guernsey cows.

```
0  20 40 60 80 100  km
0     25     50   miles
```

Above Not all the people who provide Britain with food are farmers. These fishermen are catching lobsters off the southwest coast.

Above Milking time on a dairy farm. Black-and-white Friesian cows like this give a lot of milk.

Farther north lies upland Britain: Wales, Scotland and the hills and moors of northern England. Here much of the land is impossible to plow, and the winter weather is harsh. The kind of agriculture that suits these areas best is sheep farming, and special types of sheep have been bred that do well in mountains.

Fishing used to be an important industry and fish were caught all around Britain's coasts, but now limits have been set by the EEC to avoid overfishing. Today, most fish are caught off the coasts of northeast England and eastern Scotland and in the North Sea.

17 Industry

A century ago, Great Britain was the greatest industrial nation in the world. With its coal mines, steel works and textile mills, it made goods that other countries bought eagerly.

Britain still has its traditional industries, like coal mining, but British industry itself has now changed enormously. In its dealings with foreign countries, it now buys more manufactured goods (goods made in factories) than it sells. A lot of them are goods for which Britain used to be famous, like cars. In Britain's own car industry, huge numbers of people have been made **redundant**, and the same thing has happened to many coal miners, textile-makers, and steel-workers.

But not all Britain's industries are traditional ones. An industry is anything that makes wealth. Tourism is an industry; so is entertainment, and so is helping people to manage their money — banking, financial and insurance services are now the main source of income from abroad. They are all called **service industries**. Britain's service industries are now doing much better than the old-style manufacturing industries. Britain's economy has also been helped by North Sea oil, chemicals, electronics and computers.

Top right Maintaining computers. Electronic industries like this one are Britain's new successes.

Right Traditional crafts are still important. Using all his skills, a craftsman restores an antique sofa.

Main exports:
Machinery, transportation equipment, manufactured goods, chemicals, fuels.

Main imports:
Foodstuffs, fuels, machinery, manufactured goods, chemicals.

Burning off gas on a North Sea oil rig. Britain is an important producer of oil.

18 Transportation

Above The M25, Britain's newest expressway, goes around London.

The main highway pattern in Britain is also the oldest. The road system was first created by the Roman invaders almost 2,000 years ago; in fact, some modern roads still follow the line of Roman roads. British roads and highways are today used by millions of trucks, buses and private cars. Over the past 30 years, the number of cars in Britain has soared from under 5 million to over 15 million.

Almost two-thirds of British households own private cars, but many people still rely on buses and trains. In rural areas these services are limited, so children may go to school on a special school bus.

Above It brings the mail: it also takes you where you want to go! A "postbus" on the Isle of Skye.

Railroad travel is now more difficult than it was. At the same time that road transportation was growing, Britain's railroads were being greatly reduced and many kilometers of track have been closed. However, there have been improvements as well. In modern high-speed trains, travel between Britain's big cities is much faster than it used to be. But air travel is much faster still. Britain's airports, with the huge numbers of internal and international flights they handle, are part of another transportation system that has grown enormously in a short time. In numbers of passengers, London Heathrow and London Gatwick are the largest international airports in the world.

In the past few years there has been much discussion about the building of a Channel tunnel to link Britain with mainland Europe. Plans for this "Eurotunnel" are now going ahead.

Below Waiting for their flight: some of the passengers who make Gatwick Airport the second largest international airport in the world.

The old docks in east London are now a thriving business area served by this new light railroad.

19 Government

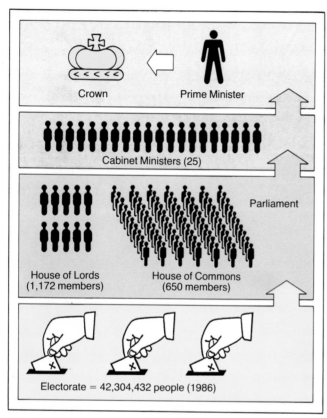

| Crown | Prime Minister |

Cabinet Ministers (25)

Parliament

House of Lords
(1,172 members)

House of Commons
(650 members)

Electorate = 42,304,432 people (1986)

Above The structure of the British government.
Below Voting at a local election: most people over the age of 18 have the vote.

Elizabeth II, Queen of Great Britain and Northern Ireland, is probably the most famous British person living today. All over the world, people have heard of her and her family. But she does not run Britain. She is the country's Head of State — and that means something different.

Britain is a **democracy**. This means that the people who live in Britain can choose the people who run the country. Every five years (it can be less), an election is held to decide who will sit in Britain's **House of Commons**. Most people over the age of 18 are allowed to vote. The men and women who are elected become Members of Parliament (MPs), and they help make the laws. Not all members of Parliament agree on how the country should be run, so they belong to different political groups, or "parties."

Most people vote for someone in one of the three largest parties — the Conservatives, the Labour (or Socialist) Party, or the Social and Liberal Democrats. The biggest party in the House of Commons holds the power and its leader is called the Prime Minister.

Right Queen Elizabeth II arriving at Westminster, with her husband, the Duke of Edinburgh, for the State opening of Parliament.

Above The Houses of Parliament in London.

Above Police officers on patrol. British police do not carry guns except in emergencies.

Among the laws Britain's governments have passed this century are many that try to help anyone who is ill, poor or out of work. Thanks to these laws Britain is a "welfare state." This means that such things as education, medical treatment and old-age pensions are paid for out of rates and taxes. In this way, being poor does not keep people from going to the doctor or going to school.

20 Facing the future

Newborn babies will hardly be in their teens before Britain enters the twenty-first century. Even in the lifetime of their parents, Britain has changed dramatically, and all Britons — young and old — are having to face the challenges that the changes have brought.

One of the most urgent challenges is unemployment. In 1987, more than 3 million British adults were out of work. The jobs they want are just not there. Unemployment is particularly bad in the north because of the decline in Britain's traditional industries. In spite of state help, being out of work means being poor, unhappy, even ill.

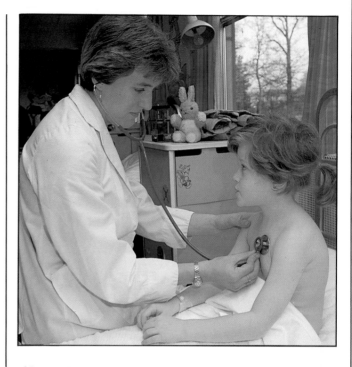

Above *Being a doctor is a top job, but most top jobs in Britain are held by men. By the time the doctor's patient grows up, British women may have won better chances of equal treatment for themselves.*

Below *Hopeful teenagers looking at the job vacancies advertised in their local job center.*

Another important challenge is the one facing Britain's farmers. The rules made by the European Economic Community have encouraged European farmers to work hard, but now they are growing more food than they can sell. In Britain, many people think that farmers should try to grow less food. This would allow the British countryside to be used for other things. More woodland could be planted. More industries could be set up that would give people jobs, and people could be given more chance to enjoy themselves in the countryside.

Above *Some of the millions of huge old trees that fell in southeast England in the 1987 storm.*

There are other worries about the environment as well. Britain, like other countries of the world, is affected by industrial pollution. To make matters worse, in October 1987, Britain was hit by the worst storm for 300 years. It is estimated that over 16 million trees were lost. It will cost millions of dollars and take many years to replace them.

The way Britain looks in the next century will depend on how well these and many other issues are handled.

Glossary

Allies   An ally is a country, person or group united with another. In World War II (1939−45) the **Allies** were Britain and the Commonwealth countries, France, the United States and the Soviet Union. They fought against Nazi Germany, Fascist Italy and Japan.

Bilingual   Speaking two languages equally well.

Carols   Christian hymns traditionally sung just before Christmas.

Colonies   Lands occupied and governed by people from another country.

Commonwealth   The association of states that are, or have at some time been, ruled by Britain. There are now 49 independent member states. Queen Elizabeth II is the Head of State in 18 of these countries, while 25 are republics.

Commuters   People who have to travel long distances to work every day.

Democracy   A form of government in which the members are elected by the people.

European Economic Community (EEC)   A group of twelve European countries that work together on many things, like trade and making laws. They are the United Kingdom of Great Britain and Northern Ireland, Eire, France, West Germany, Belgium, Luxembourg, the Netherlands, Denmark, Spain, Portugal, Italy and Greece. It is also known as the "Common Market."

Extinct   No longer existing.

Habitat   The natural home of a plant or animal.

Haggis   A traditional Scottish dish made from a mixture of lamb's liver, sheep's heart, suet, oatmeal, onions and seasoning. The ingredients are stuffed into a sheep's stomach and boiled.

House of Commons   One of the "Houses" — or sections — of Britain's Parliament. The other one is called the House of Lords. The House of Commons is made up of Members of Parliament (MPs), who are elected by the British people. The members of the House of Lords are not elected. Both Houses join in making Britain's laws.

Industrial Revolution   The great change that took place in the 1700s in the way people made things. Until then, most things were made by hand, at home. The invention of power machines meant they could be made in factories.

Mammals   Animals whose females have milk to feed their young, such as humans, sheep or cats.

Pollution   The release of substances into the air, water or land that may upset the natural balance of the environment.

Rates and taxes   Money people pay to the state to help provide services for everybody.

Redundant   Deprived of one's job because the work is no longer required by the employer.

Refugees   People who seek shelter in another country (especially to escape political or religious troubles).

Republic   A form of government without a king or queen, usually ruled by a president (such as that of France or the United States).

Service industries   People working in service industries make money by doing things for other people. Running hotels is a service industry, and so is teaching.

Suburbs   An area of housing situated away from a town or city center.

Take-away   A restaurant that sells hot take-out food to take away and eat somewhere else.

Temperate   Having a mild climate with neither very cold winters nor very hot summers.

Books to read

A Child's History of England by Charles Dickens. Biblio Distribution Centre, 1978. (reprint of 1907 edition).

Elizabeth I and Tudor England by Stephen White-Thompson. Bookwright Press, 1985.

Passport to Great Britain by Andrew Langley. Franklin Watts, 1986.

Prince Charles: Growing up in Buckingham Palace by Alma Gilleo. Child's World, 1978.

Take a Trip to England by Chris Fairclough. Franklin Watts, 1982.

Tales from English History: For Children. Agnes Strickland. Richard West, 1978.

We Live in Britain by Chris Fairclough. Franklin Watts, 1984.

Picture acknowledgments

All photographs were taken by Chris Fairclough with the exception of the following: All-Sport (UK) Ltd 13; Cephas Picture Library *cover*, 14; City Museum & Art Gallery, Birmingham 12 (top); GeoScience Features 45; Andy Hasson 30 (bottom), 44 (bottom); Michael Holford 10, 11 (bottom); Mansell Collection 11 (top); TOPHAM 32 (top right, bottom right), 43 (top); Wales Tourist Board 35 (top); Wayland Picture Library 9 (bottom), 12 (bottom), 20, 22, 26, 27 (both), 30 (top), 34; ZEFA 35 (bottom).

Index